I0437318

NO MORE ABORTIONS

NO MORE ABORTIONS

The Seed of Promise In You Is Much Too Important to Abort; SO LIVE!

BETTY J MOON

authorHOUSE®

AuthorHouse™
1663 Liberty Drive
Bloomington, IN 47403
www.authorhouse.com
Phone: 1-800-839-8640

Published by AuthorHouse   09/17/2012

ISBN: 978-1-4772-2130-3 (sc)
ISBN: 978-1-4772-2131-0 (e)

Library of Congress Control Number: 2012910659

Any people depicted in stock imagery provided by Thinkstock are models, and such images are being used for illustrative purposes only. Certain stock imagery © Thinkstock.

This book is printed on acid-free paper.

SPECIAL THANKS

To My Beloved husband Theodore Moon who always told me go for it!

My Sons, Bishop Stanley M. Williams of Fire of the Word Church, Jacksonville, Florida and Maurice Williams of Newark, New Jersey

My very special Daughter-In-Law Eunice (Dee Dee) Williams the daughter I never had.

My Sister Annette Brown, Nephew and niece Elders Aaron and Sharron Williams.

In loving of Memory:

James and Rosalie Williams (parents)

Bishop Dr. Jeff W. Banks, My late Spiritual Father in the Gospel.

Who never gave up on me? Who spoke prophetically in my life, calling those things that were!

These two women imparted wisdom in my life.

My Godmothers Mother Augusta Ellis and Mother Edith Sutton—Fluker:

INTRODUCTION

I looked in the ministry of the Lord Jesus Christ and have found that so many people are aborting their ministries. There are so many who have become weary in believing what God has called them to do for the work of the ministry. This book is to encourage you to continue to go forth and let God use you for a great work. If God has spoken a word to you, you must continue to believe that it shall come to pass. God may not come when we expect, but He will be there to fulfill the word which has been spoken into your life. Your ministry has a purpose and plan already in place that need to be fulfilled. God needs you to continue to do what you have been called to do, not just for you, but for the building of God's kingdom.

There is purpose in your life as well as your ministry. Let God use you, He will be glorified in your life. It is not by chance that He has placed a seed in you which must come forth. I speak a word in the atmosphere and say, "There shall be No More Abortions." In your life there is purpose so Live. May you be encourage and strengthen, go forth and complete the mission which God has placed upon your life.

Our father in the Name of Jesus

I pray that the person reading this book will come to understand,

That there is nothing impossible with God!

They are important to Him, and everything that concerns them.

Understanding the abortionist in there life.

The things, which holds them hostage.

Father, I pray In The Name Of Jesus, that their mind be renewed,

Their ears be opened, and their passion be rekindled,

They are released to move into their purpose and destiny! Amen

This book is about life, and about remembering who you are, not allowing what other people say or do to cause you to abort your dreams.

CONTENTS

CHAPTER 1

What is an Abortion?

Webster states: any expulsion of a fetus before it is able to survive.

> *(Being unsuccessful, fruitless, arrested in development)*

> *(To cut short as because of an equipment failure.)*

Abortion is not just limited to the physical termination of a fetus in a woman's womb.

John 10:10—The Thief cometh, but to steal, and to kills and destroy: I am come that they might have it more abundantly.

The thief comes and steals your dreams; mis-direct your passion so there is a failure in your ability to think (equipment failure). Your dreams are shut down and you lose self confidence (arrested in your development).

If we are not careful the abortionist will take up residence in our lives and we will think that it is normal to be walking in failure, self doubt; Not knowing our purpose. So we think that it's OK, and we begin to say everything is fine. You are not fine; you are dying a slow death of unhappiness, complaining and allowing circumstance and situation to swallow you up.

Ask yourself these questions; who am I? Do I have a dream? Do I have an assignment in my life? Am I a repeat offender of the same mistakes, because I am afraid to do anything else? Failure brought some shackers (uninvited guest), fear, unbelief, and self destruction. So you fear to venture out of the place where you think you are comfortable. You remain in unbelief where you no longer believe that you have the potential for purpose or destiny.

You are designed to prosper and be in health just as your soul prospers. I didn't always know that, until I began to study God' word. Not just read but study and meditate in the word of God.

When you realize, who you are then you get stirred into action, renewing your mind first. The thought process or the planning, of how you are going to prepare to get rid of the abortionist and the shackers.

You must renew your mind to the things of God it will stir up the passion for your dream, to set the goals of moving in purpose. It will change your outlook, all things will become new. The mind is the engine that stirs the spirit. You will learn by renewing your mind will change your altitude to be transformed for purpose.

Romans 12: 2

And be ye not conformed to this world: but ye are transformed by the renewing of your mind

That ye may prove what is good and acceptable and perfect, will of God.

The Will of God is his Word so by studying his word opens up your understanding to who you are in God. When you know who you are, purpose is revealed.

Free yourself from the mindset of tunnel thinking. The mind is the greatest battle ground of your potential, purpose, and destiny. Your heart is your belief system, before you can deal with change. There must be an encounter with Truth.

The most dangerous enemy to your dream is not external, but internal. Every moment of indecision will rewrite your destiny. Stop looking at the circumstances of where you are and focus on your potential! And where you are going. You must envision, dream, decide, prepare and move forward. Defeat is the result of mental blindness.

Remember your ability to think determines your living. Change your thoughts, rewrite your destiny. Getting rid of the slave mentality of I CAN'T. Or THEY WON'T LET ME (ABORTIONST) is important.

Don't ever devalue your ideas, every idea has value. In your imagination is where you see your future (future is destiny). Relationships will either abort or advance you. So be careful who you partner with. Watch out for excuses because they are poor substitutes for purpose, if you can imagine it, you can accomplish it.

Notes

CHAPTER 2

The natural pregnancies and the mirroring of spiritual pregnancies.

Ectopic pregnancy: One which develops outside the uterus, most ectopic are found in the fallopian tube, although they can occasionally occur at other pelvic sites. If a tubal pregnancy is allowed to continue, it may eventually rupture the fallopian tube and cause life threatening hemorrhage. Early diagnosis and treatment is, therefore, important, and may even allow the tube to be saved

Spiritual Ectopic Pregnancy: Some are carrying this type of baby. You are trying to be something or someone on the outside that you are not on the inside. God has to come and remove the baby before you rupture. Some think they are fine there and don't want to change, so the tube has rupture. In spite of the rupture they are afraid to allow the damage to be repaired. You must be healed before you can carry a full term to give birth.

Breech Baby: Comes out feet first. Sometimes the doctor can go in and turn the baby around.

We got our feet where we don't belong. God says pray and you want to preach, God says sing and you want to direct, God say usher and you want to nurse. We need to be turned around. We also need to ask God to order our steps. The Bible said the steps of a righteous man are ordered by God. We are turned around through seeking God's will. God will give you a strategy of how to walk in purpose to reach your destiny.

Pre-mature: Baby comes before its time. The baby is not fully developed. Something happens to make the baby come early, complications, drugs.

Spiritual pre-mature: God speaks to you and you run before you are fully prepared to go, then you ship wreck and cause others to ship wreck. You have zeal but no wisdom (instructions). You don't want to wait, we need pre-natal care to help the baby to grow and develop properly.

Ephesians 6:10-18

[10] In conclusion, be strong in the Lord [be empowered through your union with Him]; draw your strength from Him [that strength which His boundless might provides].

[11] Put on God's whole armor [the armor of a heavy-armed soldier which God supplies], that you may be able successfully to stand up against [all] the strategies *and* the deceits of the devil.

[12] For we are not wrestling with flesh and blood [contending only with physical opponents], but against the despotisms,

against the powers, against [the master spirits who are] the world rulers of this present darkness, against the spirit forces of wickedness in the heavenly (supernatural) sphere.

[13] Therefore put on God's complete armor, that you may be able to resist *and* stand your ground on the evil day [of danger], and, having done all [the crisis demands], to stand [firmly in your place].

[14] Stand therefore [hold your ground], having tightened the belt of truth around your loins and having put on the breastplate of integrity *and* of moral rectitude *and* right standing with God,

[15] And having shod your feet in preparation [to face the enemy with the [a]firm-footed stability, the promptness, and the readiness [b]produced by the good news] of the Gospel of peace.

[16] Lift up over all the [covering] shield of [c]saving faith, upon which you can quench all the flaming missiles of the wicked [one].

[17] And take the helmet of salvation and the sword that the Spirit [d]wields, which is the Word of God.

[18] Pray at all times (on every occasion, in every season) in the Spirit, with all [manner of] prayer and entreaty. To that end keep alert and watch with strong purpose *and* perseverance, interceding in behalf of all the saints (God's consecrated people). (AMP)

We need spiritual nourishment, the word of God, prayer and fasting. You need to be in a full gospel word base church, to bring correction. So you don't become a rolling stone going from church to church. You must be fed spiritually, for substance to be fortified to weather storms of life.

Notes

_____

_____

_____

_____

_____

_____

_____

_____

_____

_____

_____

_____

_____

_____

_____

_____

_____

_____

_____

_____

_____

_____

_____

_____

_____

_____

_____

CHAPTER 3

Letting go of the Past
(Getting Rid of The Residue)

Afterbirth

The placenta and the fetal membranes that are normally expelled from the uterus after the birth of the baby: Hence, the afterbirth". The placenta is of course the organ that joins the mother and the fetus and permits the provision of oxygen and nutrients to the fetus.

Hebrew 12:1-b

Let us lay aside every weight, and the sin which dose so easily beset us.

Regret' holding onto regrets. It is like dragging the weight of the past. It is always at the forefront of our mind never letting go of the hurts and disappointment, of what someone did to us. When you rehearse your past failures not only do you keep them alive, but you empower them. It has taken root. What you keep on depositing sooner or later you will make a withdrawal in your hour of weakness. It must be released from the heart. It drains our energy, leaving less available time for life in the present. We are constantly feeding the old issue.

Forgiveness is the soothing balm that can heal regret. In meditation, we can imagine discussing the issue with the self of our past and offering our forgiveness for the choice. In return we can ask ourselves for forgiveness for keeping them locked in that space for so long. Release your former self with a hug and bring forgiveness and love back into the present.

We are fertile ground for new seeds to be planted and new dreams to be birth.

Get rid of the residue of the past, failure, and heartbreak. Church hurt. Stop recreating the situation in your mind. Sometimes you have to change places to give birth, because you are not in a healthy place to give birth.

In the word of God Hebrews 8:12 Their Sins . . . . Will I Remember No More"

Your past is your past. Do you guilt trip over your past? Is God forgetful? No He chooses not to remember our sins and you choose other wise. You are walking in doubt of what God's word says and you forfeit the confidence needed to pray for and receive what God has for you.

Shame is not a blessing, it is a weight that Jesus carried to the cross, so set it down and walk away. You have the right to do that because God's promise is as far as the east is from the west, so far hath he removed our transgressions from us. Any time the devil brings up the past it's because he hopes we are ignorant to the truth, he fears your future; he wants to rob you of God's best.

You got to have strong faith and use it to win. Everybody has a problem, or they live with one. This means everybody suffers at one time or another suffers losses, misunderstood, forsaken, and alone.

Expand your capacity of believe. Because one moment of fear will cause you to abort; one moment of Faith will create miracles. Purpose will keep you alive, press through your issues.

Notes

_____

_____

_____

_____

_____

_____

_____

_____

_____

_____

_____

_____

_____

_____

_____

_____

_____

_____

_____

_____

_____

_____

_____

_____

_____

_____

_____

_____

_____

CHAPTER 4

I Almost Aborted

I woke up in the middle of the night. I couldn't sleep so I went to the living room and laid on the couch and dosed off. I heard the Holy Spirit speak and say JoAnne No More Abortions. I said The Blood of Jesus loose here devil and laid back down. I heard it again JoAnne No More Abortions. I sat up and said devil you are a liar I am not pregnant. I laid back down and this time I felt some one shake my foot I thought it was my husband. I sat up looked around and saw no one. I knew it was the Lord speaking to me. I said Lord I'm not pregnant with a baby.

The Holy Spirit said yes you are with my word. I began to repent and repent. I poured my heart out to the Lord.

I was going through so many changes. My spiritual father had just passed away about a year or two ago and I didn't have time to properly mourn him. He was the only real pastor I ever had.

Bishop Banks had mentored me and also my sons as a natural and spiritual father. Bishop Banks had spoken prophetically in my life. He never threw you away; even in your worst state he loved you back. He mirrored the love of God to the hurting and wounded with compassion. He saw the potential and nurtured it. He spoke to it and called it forth. That was my first encounter with a real prophet.

Being complacent in the body I had just stopped functioning in ministry. I was just going through the motion of church. What I couldn't understand is people who I thought knew their purpose really didn't know nor did they walk in any authority. They were going along with any boat that floated. I just didn't understand. Well the Holy Ghost shook me and spoke to me and said I have invested too much in you. You are about to abort what I have impregnated you with.

There are families, not just men and women in you. Get up and push; Give Birth! Do not abort the prophecy that was spoken over you and the impartation by the laying on of hands."

My mind drifted to 2 Timothy 1:6 Wherefore I put thee in remembrance that thou stir up the gift of God, which is in thee by the putting on of my hands.

Paul was encouraging Timothy to be faithful to his legacy of faith. Paul knows this faith lives in Timothy. This gift of faith has also been imparted to you. So fan the flame of the gift of God which is in you through the laying on of hands.

2 Timothy 1:7 God did not give us the Spirit of fear, but the spirit of power, of love and of a sound mind.

When Paul told Timothy to fan the flame, He implied that Gifts are not given in full bloom, but that they need to be developed.

Clearly Timothy's spiritual gift had been given to him when Paul and the Elders had laid their hands on him and set him apart for ministry.

The Holy Spirit was telling me to persevere. I did not need a new revelation or new gifts; I need the courage and self discipline to hang on to the truth and use the gifts. I had already received. If I would step out boldly in faith and proclaim the good news once again.

The Holy Spirit would go with me. My late Bishop Banks had laid hands on me and spoke in my life.

The Lord began to let me see babies that were yet in the birthing canal that had not been pushed out. There were some who were born, but yet left on their own with no nurturing.

The Holy Spirit began to deal with me about the word abortion; about how generations were being aborted right in the church and no one could see they were dying in the pew. This is a result of no one speaking to their potential only preaching at them and not to them. No one is imparting; no one calling forth the God man or the God woman. They needed to know they are somebody in the body of Christ and that God really has a purpose for them. Helping them to understand, their gifting or their call to grow into who God has called them to be. I began to say God I don't have anyone to help me, because I felt deserted by my family and church family.

I sounded like the man by the pool of Bethesda. Everything seemed to have been turned upside down. I was going to leave. I had been offered a pastorship at a small church the people seemed to care for me I was sitting in a restaurant one night convincing myself why I should leave.

This man of God came out of the blue and said God said go back home for you have been planted in that house.

God has impregnated you with a word (NO MORE ABORTIONS). Well you could have knocked me over with a feather.

What you hear in your spirit from the Lord must be tested by the Word of God and by the Spirit and by practicality. I continued to seek God. He confirmed the word he had spoke to me, so I stepped out on Faith with a lot of confrontation. You would have thought the word abortion was something against society.

I recruited my godchildren and did my first conference at the Restoration Center in Newark, New Jersey. It had a men's shelter attached to it and each night some of the men came and received the word, the last night my church family came, I was so elated until I had the glad, glad. Prophet Robert Bryant from Maryland came and spoke a prophetic release over the church and property; within the next week at lest 25 of those men began to find jobs went to school and found apartments. They were about to abort their purpose. There was a preacher in hiding who had given up, but they went back home to fulfill his purpose.

I had to get rid of the residue in my life in order to carry out my assignment. People must realize the spirit in you that is what you administer out to who ever you are ministering to; if it is hurt then hurt is speaking to them subliminally.

Church hurt is the worst hurt you can have especially by people who act as if they never seen you before and go along with the wrong. I suffered in silence every night I told God he had deserted me and I asked him why. I said God I did just what you told me to do, I was faithful to you and leadership, if I did anything wrong tell me so I can correct it. I gave God my resume as if he didn't know I said God I stayed when everyone else walked off and took the reducible, and was treated like we were a people without a vision wandering in the wilderness, yet God was silent.

Notes

_____

_____

_____

_____

_____

_____

_____

_____

_____

_____

_____

_____

_____

_____

_____

_____

_____

_____

_____

_____

_____

_____

_____

_____

_____

_____

_____

_____

_____

_____

CHAPTER 5

Seed Faith

I began to think back about when I was a little girl with polio, how my mother sowed seeds into Oral Roberts Ministries for my healing and believed God after the doctors said I would never walk again. I learned about seed sowing at a young age and how powerful a seed can be when it is planted in the right ground. When you sow seed you must give your seed an assignment. Before we were our assignment was already assigned we were pre-destined to be great in God and do great and mighty things. In being called, we have to realize.

With God Nothing is Impossible!

If I Perish, I perish (Esther 4:16)

Nothing great is done for God without sacrifice, until someone does some giving.

After the decree, to kill the Jews was given. Mordicai and Esther could have despaired; and decided to save only themselves or just waited for Gods intervention. Instead they saw that God had placed them in their positions for a purpose, so they seized the moment and devised a plan.

Queen Esther knew this, When Mordicai told her of the wicked Haman's intention to annihilate all the Jews. She went into action. She asked her people to fast and pray. She prepared herself to go before the king and petition him.

Now Esther had not been summoned by the King for months, and to go unbidden, was a no no. She might have been put to death. Her only hope was for the king to extend his scepter. But Esther was ready to risk everything to save her people. She mentally sacrificed herself when she cried, If I perish, I perish! This is real giving.

When Esther went before the King, God touched his heart. He extended the scepter to her and spared her life.

Because Esther was willing to sacrifice everything. She was able to save her people from extinction.

That was something big! But don't forget, Esther did something big for God first!

Do you want God to do something big in your life? Something spiritually? Financially? Then be willing to do something big for God. Take The First Bold Step!

When you have challenges in life seek to know what God wants you to do and then do it. Be confident that he will do his part. You don't know a head of time how he will accomplish his will, Trust God and prepare to be surprised by the way he demonstrates his trustworthiness. God may have placed you where you are.

FOR SUCH A TIME AS THIS!

Notes

_____

_____

_____

_____

_____

_____

_____

_____

_____

_____

_____

_____

_____

_____

_____

_____

_____

_____

_____

_____

_____

_____

_____

_____

_____

_____

_____

_____

_____

_____

_____

CHAPTER 6

What do you do when God is silent?

I did what I knew how to do, I talked to God as the Daddy I knew him to be to me. I praised and worshiped him I heard the Holy Spirit wooing me I will meet You at the Alter of your heart. I began to sing a song I don't know if some one had wrote that song or not but that comforted me at that moment.

The alter is where God will change you because Your heart must be altered in order for God's Glory to be manifested through you. The more I worship God, the more he loved on me and the love of God cleansed my heart and brought true deliverance; for me to forgive. Only Gods love can cause true forgiveness. I just wanted to stay in his presences didn't want to leave. But I had an assignment.

I got up washed my faced and began to speak to my spirit. You are more than a conqueror, so why are you cast down O my soul Hope thou in God. My song became Lord I Trust You, because you have made me to be, Armed and Dangerous and Highly Favored by the most High God. This became my confession.

I learned to trust God through my hurt, my pain and the storm in my life at that time.

I had been wounded in the house of the Lord, I could hear in my spirit the voice of my late Bishop Banks (never let them see you sweat). I also stood on the word of God. If God spoke it to me I didn't care who didn't believe. I held fast to the word of God.

You can't waiver into unbelief don't look at the situation look at the finish product. If you can see it in your mind then you can make it happen.

I began to see men, women, boys and girls being birthed into the kingdom of God with great gifts and talents, not just looking at the art but, becoming artist of the gospel, and also fisher's of men and demonstrating the kingdom of God.

Mid-wives were in place. They had been trained to birth the babies and then passed on to fathers and mothers who nurtured and properly groomed them for kingdom work.

God had already told me what to do I just had to do it and trust God. I learned God did not speak to me again until it was time for the next phase in my life.

I still don't know why God has me where I am. So I just stay and be obedient to my father because it Is better then our so called sacrifice.

There is nothing like God, my Daddy, loving on you and making things up where you have been humiliated. There is nothing like the love of God.

Notes

_____

_____

_____

_____

_____

_____

_____

_____

_____

_____

_____

_____

_____

_____

_____

_____

_____

_____

_____

_____

_____

_____

_____

_____

_____

_____

CHAPTER 7

When Other's Forget, God Remembers

Early in my life when I had polio I would watch Oral Roberts on TV in the 50's. He would be preaching and laying hands on people and say Be Healed in Jesus Name.

One Day I was watching him and I put my hands on the TV and I was standing on my crutches the power of God knock me down and my mother came running in the living room and said what happen I couldn't explain it. Now I know it was the power of God. I told God back then I wanted to be just like Oral Roberts laying hand on the sick. I wanted to be used by God. Soon after that the doctor took the crutches an gave me some ugly special made shoes with braces I had to wear them to school and kids would tease me and call me cripple, my brother Aaron would beat them up.

One day I told my gym teacher Mr. Cook I could walk without these old ugly braces, he smiled and said I bet you could. That night I told God I was tried of those ugly shoes. He said take them off I did and I walked in the living room barefooted. You could have knocked my mother and father over with a feather. Great is Our God! My mother called every body and told everybody about my miracle.

I began to pray and ask God what you want me to do

It might seem strange that I that I was having a conversation with God and he spoke back to me. See you have to be in relationship with him and study his word so you will understand how he talks. When I was young My Godmother Sister Ellis would read the Bible to us so it was not hard to believe when I heard that God could heal me. Being taught to pray is a learned behavior. But having, Faith that God can do anything, But Fail.

When I was coming up my grandmother would tell stories of family history. How God healed through a cousin she was an evangelist that traveled doing revivals where blind eyes were open, cancer healed and limb grew out. There is a history of relationship with God in my family of knowing that God can!

Mark 9:23

If thou canst believe. All things are possible to him that believeth.   (KJV)

Notes

_____

_____

_____

_____

_____

_____

_____

_____

_____

_____

_____

_____

_____

_____

_____

_____

_____

_____

_____

_____

_____

_____

_____

_____

_____

_____

_____

_____

_____

_____

CHAPTER 8

You Must Forgive:

Forgiveness is the mental and or spiritual process of ceasing to feel resentment, indignation or anger against another person for a preconceived offense, indifference or mistake, or ceasing to demand punishment or restitution. Forgive and forget!

Forgiveness is the key to action and freedom, forgiveness is the scent that the rose leaves on the heel that crushes it. This is certain that a person that studies revenge keeps his wounds green, which otherwise would heal and do well. To err is human, to forgive is divine.

Resentment is one burden that is incompatible with success. Always be first to forgive; and forgive yourself always.

It is not uncommon for people to have questions about forgiveness. Forgiveness doesn't come easy for most of us. Our natural instinct is to put up a wall of protection when or after we've been injured.

We just don't automatically forgive when we have been done wrong. The Bible tells us to forgive as God has forgiven us.

(Colossians 3:13—Forbearing one another and forgiving one another, if any man have quarrel against any; even as Christ forgave you also do ye.)

When you forgive it empowers you to do the will of God and to walk in purpose. When you don' forgive you are held hostage in your own fear of hurt and that person has your Key to destiny.

It also distracts your mind from purpose and achievement and keeps you from tapping into your potential. Let It Go! Renew Your Mind and Rekindle Your Passion.

Take the power from the person who has hurt you. If you don't let go they have power over you.

When you do as the Bible say it will not only free you, but everything and every person that is connected to you. If your brother or sister think you have wronged them apologize quickly.

Notes

CHAPTER 9

Understanding The Process of Change
(To recognize the hidden ability and potential)

Genesis 38 &39 Joseph

Having big dreams is great. God wants us to have big dreams, but we must realize there is a process that we must go through in order to accomplish those dreams.

Every person God used mightily in the Bible went through a process. Consider Joseph in the Old Testament. The anointing of God was upon his life and he was highly favored, yet what a process he went through from the pit to the palace. Joseph was a dreamer who became ruler over Egypt. He went through a process.

The first key to seeing your dreams come true is to be focused and to recognize that you have purpose and appreciate the opportunity given at that time.

In Genesis 39, we see that Joseph gave the utmost care to what was entrusted to him. (Verses 2-6) states the Lord was with Joseph and he prospered, and he lived in the house of his Egyptian master. When the master saw that the Lord was with him and gave him success in everything he did, Joseph had favor and became his attendant.

When Gods anointing is upon you the devil (abortionist) will try to cause you to abort the purpose and destiny.

You must stay focused to fulfill your purpose (dream) to manifestation.

Potipher put Joseph in charge of his whole household and everything he owned. Potipher's wife tried to seduce Joseph, but he refused and she lied on him and said he tried to rape her. When he was falsely accused this was part of the process for Joseph.

Joseph was faithful with what was placed in his hands and waited until such a time that God raised him to the next level.

Watch Out For The Thief

The Thief cometh not, but for to steal and to kill, and to destroy I am come that they might have life. And that they might have it more abundantly.

John 10:10

The thief come for this reason to take your life, most people would instantly think that this life of this stealing, killing and destroying you physically. He does something far worse then that, he comes to steal and destroy your consciousness (abortionist).

You open the door for the devil by your thought pattern, what you create and entertain. The thief (devil) introduces false concepts about being poor.

Genesis: 1:27-28 (KJV)

(God) created man in his own image, in the image of God created he him; male and female created he them. And God blessed them God said unto them Be fruitful and multiply and replenish the earth. And subdue it and have dominion over the fish of the sea and over the fowl of the air and over every living thing that move upon the earth. If we were truly poor then that would mean that God is poor also. Because were created in his image. Nothing about God spells welfare. Poverty is a state of mind, a false concept that the thief implanted with your permission.

Notes

CHAPTER 10

Who are you?

Proverbs 23:7-A, For as he think in his heart, so is he.

Being confident in God, knowing who you are, and who God is in you.

Let's take a look at a tree for instant. When fall comes the tree begin to drop her leaves by the time winter comes the tree is ready when spring time comes around the tree begin to blossom.

It is a principle of seedtime and harvest. Because the tree is bare in the winter dose not mean that it's barren and unfruitful.

In the Fall is the season when the sap leaves the branches and drains to the roots to strengthen the tree for the winter. When the trees drop their leaves they don't save any for next year they let it all fall to the ground. They will get it all back and more.

The principle of seedtime and harvest, when you sow you will reap.

Jeremiah 17: 8

For he shall be as a tree planted by the waters, and that spreadeth out her roots by the river, and shall not see when heat cometh, but her leaf shall be green: and shall not be careful in the year of drought, neither shall cease from yielding fruit.

Notes

_____

_____

_____

_____

_____

_____

_____

_____

_____

_____

_____

_____

_____

_____

_____

_____

_____

_____

_____

_____

_____

_____

_____

_____

_____

_____

_____

_____

CHAPTER 11

The death and rebirth of Self

Sometimes a part of us must die before another part can come to life.

Even though this is a natural and necessary part of our growth, it is often painful or, if we don't realize what's happening, confusing and disorienting.

In fact, confusion and disorientation are often the messengers that tell us a shifting or change happens throughout the lives of all humans, as we move from infancy to childhood to adolescence and beyond. With each transition from one phase to another, we find ourselves saying good-bye to an old friend, the identity that we formed in order to move through that particular time.

Now it is in the hour of revealing the true You

Example: The death of the skin between a fetus' fingers that causes webbing, as the hand grow into what we recognize as precious infant hands, the cells that make up the web-like structures between each finger of the fetus disintegrate.

What was suitable for one stage of development or function may not be enough to carry us successfully through the higher stage of our destiny.

I want to leave this thought with you (The seed of equivalent benefit).

The seed of equivalent benefit, in other words, in every mistake you make in life, God has placed another seed. If you know the seed is there it will nullify that mistake or it will give you something greater to take its place."

The seed of equivalent faith is more than learning the hard way through hindsight. It is God's way of turning your defeat into benefits, your failure into successes. And if you apply what you have learned. You nullify the mistake. It's like a new beginning.

Notes

Our Father in the Name of Jesus,

I thank you!

For the person, that has read this book and has been energized to persevere, to overcome the abortionist, in their life.

To know the challenges of life is just a stepping stone to purpose and destiny.

They move with the tenacity, building a momentum for an impact of life!

Amen!

FAMOUS QUOTES BY UNSUNG HEROES

THE LATE DR. BISHOP JEFF W. BANKS:

IF YOU BELIEVE IT, YOU CAN RECEIVE IT, BUT IF YOU DOUBT IT,

YOU WILL BE WITHOUT!

BISHOP STANLEY M. WILLIAMS:

IF YOU GOT THE FAITH! GOD GOT THE POWER!

BETTY J MOON:

NO MORE ABORTIONS!

Elder AARON WILLIAMS JR.:

RELEASE YOURSELVE!

BISHOP GREGORY A. WOODS:

WATCH ME LIVE!